# Son of a Bitch

**Anna Morris**

W0038014

*methuen* | drama

LONDON • NEW YORK • OXFORD • NEW DELHI • SYDNEY

METHUEN DRAMA

Bloomsbury Publishing Plc, 50 Bedford Square, London, WC1B 3DP, UK
Bloomsbury Publishing Inc, 1385 Broadway, New York, NY 10018, USA
Bloomsbury Publishing Ireland, 29 Earlsfort Terrace, Dublin 2,
D02 AY28, Ireland

BLOOMSBURY, METHUEN DRAMA and the Methuen
Drama logo are trademarks of Bloomsbury Publishing Plc.

First published in Great Britain 2025

Photographer: Karla Gowlett

Designer: Katie Gabriel Allen

A catalogue record for this book is available from the British Library.

A catalog record for this book is available from the Library of Congress.

ISBN: PB: 978-1-3505-5822-9
ePDF: 978-1-3505-5823-6
eBook: 978-1-3505-5824-3

Series: Modern Plays

Typeset by Mark Heslington Ltd, Scarborough, North Yorkshire

For product safety related questions contact productsafety@bloomsbury.com.

To find out more about our authors and books visit
www.bloomsbury.com and sign up for our newsletters.

# SON OF A BITCH

## By Anna Morris

*Son of a Bitch* premiered at the Edinburgh Festival Fringe at Summerhall on 1 August 2024. It was produced by The Thelmas in association with Josie Underwood and directed by Madelaine Moore. The play won a Fringe First Award for outstanding new writing.

The production transferred to Southwark Playhouse on 26 February 2025, produced by The Thelmas and Side Quest Productions, directed by Madelaine Moore and supported by Arts Council England.

**Edinburgh Fringe Summerhall 2024**
**Creative and Production Team**

The Thelmas in association with Josie Underwood present

# SON OF A BITCH

## By Anna Morris

**Cast:** Anna Morris

**Director:** Madelaine Moore

**Dramaturg:** David Jackson

**Sound Designer:** Ellie Isherwood

**Lighting Designer:** Megan Lucas

**Technical Stage Manager:** Josie Shipp

**Producers:** The Thelmas in association with Josie Underwood

**Executive Producer:** Danny Willis

**BSL Interpreter:** Shaurna Dickson

**Press:** Storytelling PR

# SUMMERHALL

Southwark Playhouse 2025
Creative and Production Team

The Thelmas and Side Quest Productions present

# SON OF A BITCH

## By Anna Morris

**Cast:** Anna Morris

**Director:** Madelaine Moore

**Dramaturg:** David Jackson

**Set Designer:** Cory Shipp

**Sound Designer:** Ellie Isherwood

**Associate Sound Designer:** Bella Kear

**Lighting and Creative Captioning Designer:** Megan Lucas

**Production Manager:** Brent Tan

**Technical Stage Manager:** Leigh Arthur

**Producers:** The Thelmas and Side Quest Productions

**Press:** Mobius PR

**Marketing:** Cup of Ambition

## Anna Morris | Writer and Actor

Anna Morris is an award-winning comedian, actress and writer. For TV she played Sophie, Duchess of Edinburgh in Channel 4's *The Windsors* and starred as Pippa in Channel 4 comedy drama *Lee and Dean*. She's also featured in BBC sitcoms: *Outnumbered*, *Count Arthur Strong*, *The First Team* and ITV's comedy entertainment show *Bad Bridesmaid*, which she also wrote.

For the stage, she's written five one-woman character comedies which have received critical acclaim and had sell-out runs in the UK and Australia: *Dolly Mixture*, *Would Like to Thank*, *It's Got to be Perfect* and most recently *Bitchelors* and *Bombastic* which both ran at the Soho Theatre. Her BBC Radio 4 comedy special *Kid-Life Crisis* aired and became a stand-up show at the Edinburgh Fringe in 2022. *Son of a Bitch* is her debut play and is currently in development for TV.

Anna has single sided deafness and advocates access for sign language users and audiences with hearing and sight impairments. All performances at the Southwark Playhouse will have integrated creative captioning and the run will include three British Sign Language (BSL) interpreted performances.

## Madelaine Moore | Director

Madelaine Moore is an award-winning stage and screen director, and one half of The Thelmas. Twice shortlisted for the Sir Peter Hall Director's Award and an Old Vic 12 Director, her work is informed by her interest in disrupting traditional gendered narratives.

Madelaine's debut short film as writer/director, *Twitching*, was selected for multiple International film festivals (including BAFTA and BIFA qualifying festivals), nominated for Best Screenplay at Little Venice Film Festival and won the Audience Award for Best UK Film at Poppy Jasper International Film Festival in 2023.

Theatre credits include: *The Ice at the End of the World* (Omnibus); *OUTPATIENT* (Summerhall, Reading Rep and The Lowry); *Glacier* (Old Fire Station); *Edith* (Lowry and Theatr Clwyd); *Gobble Gobble Gobble Gobble Goblin* (Old Vic Theatre); *Ladykiller* (national tour, Brits Off Broadway); *Evelyn* (Mercury Theatre, Southwark Playhouse); *Second Person Narrative* (Arcola Theatre); *The Awakening* (Jack Studio); *Algorithms* (Soho Theatre, Park Theatre, Netflix Stage to Screen winner); *Santi & Naz* (Soho Theatre and national tour, Charlie Hartill winner).

## David Jackson | Dramaturg

David Jackson is a freelance writer and director. He has written for ITV, BBC Radio 4 and the National Youth Theatre. He directed and co-wrote *The Eulogy of Toby Peach* (winner: The IdeasTap Underbelly award, Edinburgh Fringe), which was performed at the VAULT Festival (winner: Pick of the Week Award) and then transferred to the Criterion Theatre.

David also directed and co-wrote Anna Morris's sell out show *It's Got to be Perfect* (winner: Funny Women Award, Best Show 2016). He devised and directed *Welcoming the World* at the National Theatre as part of the National Youth Theatre's contribution to the 2012 Olympics. He has also written several plays performed at the Edinburgh Fringe, Brighton Fringe and in London.

## Cory Shipp | Set Designer

Cory Shipp is a set and costume designer working across all ranges of performative work across the UK. Cory trained at the Royal Welsh College of Music and Drama.

Theatre (as designer) includes: *The Mikvah Project* (Orange Tree Theatre); *Cyrano de Bergerac, Easy Virtue* (The Watermill Theatre); *Mr Burns: A Post-Electric Play, RENT, Return to the Forbidden Planet, Vinegar Tom, Caucasian Chalk Circle, 6 Characters* (Mountview Theatre Academy); *Justice in a Day* (Theatr Clwyd); *Hags* (Scratchworks Theatre Company); *Boy, Blue Stockings, Tristan and Yseult, Much Ado About Nothing, Alice in Wonderland* (LAMDA); *Cinderella* (The Barn Theatre); *Pilgrims* (Guildhall); *Spring Awakening* (Leeds Conservatoire); *Anyone Can Whistle* (Southwark Playhouse); *Deffro'r Gwanwyn* (Y Cwmni); *Glacier* (Old Fire Station); *The EU Killed My Dad* (Jermyn Street Theatre); *The Book of Eternity* (Northern Opera); *Pontypool* (Wales Millennium Centre) and *A Role to Die For* (Barn Theatre).

Theatre (as costume designer) includes: *Unfortunate: A Musical Parody* (Fat Rascal Theatre Company/Underbelly Festival); *Bandstand, Sweeney Todd* (ArtsEd); *Big Fish* (Mountview).

Theatre (as set designer) includes: *Wipe These Tears* (Bezna Theatre Company); *Justice in a Day* (Theatr Clwyd); *Sweet Charity* (ArtsEd); *The Lion, The B!tch and The Wardrobe* (Wales Millennium Centre).

### Ellie Isherwood | Sound Designer

Ellie Isherwood is a sound designer, composer, actor/musician and synth-pop artist (BYFYN). Her 'quietly ground breaking' work spans a vast array of forms, from site specific theatre to binaural audio experiences to musical theatre. Recent work includes composition and sound design for *Tender* (Bush Theatre); *The Fir Tree* (Arts Depot); *The Odyssey* (Unicorn Theatre); *The Intrusion* (Leeds Playhouse).

## Megan Lucas | Lighting and Creative Captioning Designer

Megan Lucas is a lighting and video designer. She has a personal interest in accessible theatre and as a result she developed and programmed a custom low cost hard-of-hearing captioning system, most recently used at the Taking the Stage festival in Milton Keynes.

Lighting designer credits include: *Street of Crocodiles* (Tring Park); *Ice at the End of the World* (Omnibus); *Lynn Faces* (Summerhall and UK tour); *Son of a Bitch* (Summerhall, Southwark Playhouse); *OUTPATIENT* (Summerhall, Reading Rep and The Lowry); *Fade* (Lowry/Leeds Playhouse); *Bert's House* (UK tour); *Stray Dogs* (Theatre503); *The Hidden Garden* (National Opera Studio); *Edie* (Theatre503); *Criptic Pit Party* (The Barbican); *The Masks We Wear* (Royal and Derngate).

Assistant lighting designer credits include: *How the Other Half Loves* (Salisbury Playhouse); *Much Ado About Nothing* (National Theatre); *Alcina* (Glyndebourne).

Relighter credits include: *Wuthering Heights* (UK tour).

Video designer credits include: *OUTPATIENT* (Summerhall, Reading Rep and The Lowry); *We Started to Sing* (Arcola Theatre); *The Wellspring* (Royal and Derngate/UK tour).

## Leigh Arthur | Technical Stage Manager

Leigh Arthur is an Irish freelance technical stage manager and musician based in London.

She has a background in TV and film production, having worked for Sony Pictures, Teenage Cancer Trust and Sixteen Films, as well as directing music videos for acts in Ireland, the UK and Germany. Leigh has a love for storytelling, with an emphasis on elevating underrepresented and outsider voices.

TSM credits include: *Unseen* (UK tour); *You're So F\*\*king Croydon* (Underbelly, Edinburgh); *Juniper and Jules* (Pleasance); *Dave Hill's Caveman in a Spaceship* (Soho Theatre); *Algorithms* (Park Theatre).

Lighting design for *Big Joanie* (Third Man Records) at Southbank Festival curated by Chaka Khan and *for Special Interest* (Rough Trade Records) at 90 Mil, Berlin.

## Brent Tan | Production Manager

Brent Tan is a Singaporean born producer/production manager/stage manager based in the UK. Brent's interests are in immersive and touring productions.

Theatre credits include, as Production Manager: *The Lonesome Death of Eng Bunker* (Omnibus Theatre); *Commons Dance Festival* (Stanley Arts, London); *Wish You Weren't Here* (Theatre Centre/UK tour).

As Stage Manager: *Wonderland in Alice* (Octagon Theatre*);* *Animal Farm the Musical* and *50 Days* (Birmingham Hippodrome); *1884* (ConeyHQ, Shoreditch/Brighton); *Home X* (Barbican Theatre); Bunker of Zion (UK tour); *WeRNotVirus2* (Moongate Theatre/Omnibus Theatre); *Amaterasu: Out of the Cave* (Arcola Theatre).

As Company Stage Manager: *Tones* (WoundUp Theatre on tour); *Richard the Second* (Tangle Theatre/UK tour); as Technical Stage Manager, *Talawa First* (Talawa Theatre); as Deputy Stage Manager, *Get Happy* (Barbican Centre/Stoke-on-Trent); and, as Technical Manager, *Prague Quadrennial* (Secretive Thing, Prague).

## Guleraana Mir | Producer

Guleraana Mir is an award-winning writer and theatre maker, and one half of The Thelmas. She is passionate about telling authentic stories that celebrate not stereotype, and speak to complex social realities in a fresh and disruptive way.

She specialises in developing new work through devising and writing with young people and community groups, and leads writing programmes for artists of all ages at a number of institutions including National Theatre and Royal Central School of Speech and Drama.

Guleraana is currently working on her first mainstage play and has an original TV series in development with afshan d'souza-lodhi.

Writing credits include: *Santi & Naz* (co-writer with afshan d'souza-lodhi, Soho Theatre and national tour); *At What Cost?, Take A Chance On Me, The Testing Place* for BBC's *Doctors* (Series 24); *All the Small Things* (BBC Children's); *Misfits* (co-writer, Queen's Theatre Hornchurch); *The Bigger Picture* (audio, commissioned by Tamasha and SOAS) and *COCONUT* (Ovalhouse and national tour).

## The Thelmas

The Thelmas is an award-winning female-led theatre company established to develop and promote female-led artistic work that gives space to marginalised voices. We do this by telling playfully disruptive stories that appeal to diverse audiences and bridge the gap between the political and the mainstream. Our work is thought-provoking, complex and boisterous. Through our public productions, community-building and women-centred workshops, we explore the social, political and cultural stories that matter in fresh and surprising ways.

Their productions include *COCONUT* by Guleraana Mir (Ovalhouse and national tour 2018); *Ladykiller* by Madeline Gould (Pleasance 2018, VAULT 2019, national tour and Brits Off Broadway selection 2020); *Notch* by Danaja Wass (VAULT 2020); *Santi & Naz* (VAULT 2020, Pleasance 2023, national tour 2024 and Soho Theatre 2025); *Son of a Bitch* by Anna Morris (Summerhall 2024, Southwark Playhouse 2025).

The company is led by director, Madelaine Moore and writer, Guleraana Mir.

## Side Quest Productions

Side Quest Productions is a production company for stage and screen led by director Madelaine Moore. Side Quest brings stories from the outer limits to the mainstream be that thematically, politically or theatrically; a good night out in the left of field, designed to provoke and entertain.

## THANKS

To my incredible family for supporting my creative endeavours (which began at the age of eight when I performed a puppet show in school – credit must be given to my teacher Mrs Eleanor Jones for being my first reviewer). Mum, Dad, Kate, Alex, Will, Henry, Daisy and my partner-in-crime Sam Underwood – I love you all loads.

To my incredible 'Wizardish' Cousin Steven Frampton and Mark Grayson for their support.

Thank you to my director and producer Madelaine Moore who replied to my initial email in February 2024 to say 'this sounds like a fantastic premise for a show! Let me give it a read' and subsequently agreed to direct *Son of a Bitch*. To Guleraana Mir, the other half of The Thelmas, and Josie Underwood – who came on board to produce the play for the Edinburgh Festival Fringe.

To all of the creatives in Edinburgh and Southwark who have helped bring Marnie's world to life. This has been such a collaborative effort and I'm so proud of what we've created as a team.

Thank you to Tom Forster at Summerhall for programming the play for the Edinburgh Fringe, and to Southwark Playhouse for transferring it to London.

Dave Jackson, my dramaturg – thank you for being such a brilliant creative accomplice and great friend. Your contribution to my creative journey has played a huge part in how I got here.

To every single person who contributed to the Crowdfunder to help get this show to the Edinburgh Fringe and my executive producer Danny Willis. I am so grateful to every single one of you.

To my A-Level Theatre Studies teacher Angie Morris, for helping me believe in myself.

To all of my incredible friends for their support, love and encouragement – especially when times have been tough and I've felt like giving up.

Shout-out to the following groups: The Theatre Gals, Lady C\*\*ts, Bingle Bangles, Hitchin Writers Group, The DND Cat Coven, Thornden/BP Girls, The Pussy Club, Peach People, Clearcast, Hitchin Pantry, Worldweary-but-heroic Female Comics, Edinburgh Solo Support Group, Edinburgh Flatmates 2024!

**In loving memory of Kerry McIntosh:**

**your creativity, resilience and strength continues to inspire me and many others.**

# SON OF A BITCH

**mother**

*(noun)*
   a woman in relation to her child or children.

*(verb)*
   bring up (a child) with care and affection.

**Google's English dictionary provided by Oxford Languages.**

For my sister, Kate
*(for always believing)*

# Son of a Bitch

**Cast**

**Marnie**, *early forties (plays all of the characters)*

*(,) symbolises a beat/a pause.*

**Scene One**

**Pilot** (*V/O*)   Cabin crew prepare for take-off.

**Marnie** *is standing, watching a video on her phone.*

*We can't see the video, but we can hear distorted snippets. An altercation with cabin crew, a plane engine, a child screaming. We hear* **Marnie** *shout –*

**Marnie** (*audio*)   Shut the fuck up you little cu–

*Blackout.*


**Scene Two**

*Lights up.*

**Marnie**   Well, this is awkward.

(,)

I assume you've seen the video?

If you haven't – it's still available on all platforms.

Apparently it's also on TikTok as a sea shanty.

(,)

Seven words. Ten seconds.

I am hung, drawn and quartered in 280 characters.

In five-second cut downs.

I became a gif.

A meme.

A bitch.

A witch.

A warning?

In the childfree world – I become an influencer.

For contraception.

(,)

Morning TV shows hastily make features:

'Are some women just bad mothers?'

(,)

Yes. No?

If that's what you think.

What do *you* think?

(,)

I catch the end of a women's chat show.

**Presenter**    I'm sorry but women *like this* should just be sterilised.

**Marnie**    I try Radio 4.

**Woman**    As a mother of three, I am sickened!

I would adopt him – if I hadn't already taken in a Ukrainian family.

**Marnie**    A man phoned in – even though it's that show where women are supposed to get their own hour.

**Man**    As a father who does the majority of childcare in our house, I'm wondering where her husband is in all of this?

He should get custody . . . and a restraining order.

**Marnie**    A representative from Mumsnet jumps in.

**Mumsnet Woman**    Well, we don't know her circumstances. It *is* possible to suffer from post-natal depression many years after birth.

**Marnie**    Nope. No post-natal depression.

Sorry to disappoint you.

I am . . . *I was . . .*

Perfectly sane.

(,)

So how do you feel about me now?


**Scene Three**

**Airport** (*V/O*)    Ladies and gentlemen, this is a safety announcement. Please do not leave any unattended luggage in the baggage area.

**Marnie** *is scrolling through her phone.*

**Marnie**    I found out I was 'famous' while having an IBS attack in Heathrow Airport.

At 9.30am.

In a toilet cubicle.

(*Holds phone.*) Airplane mode off.

*SFX: Message notification ping. Ping ping ping.*

I thought someone had died.

My friend Lucy

**Lucy**    Marnie, what the fuck is going on? Have you checked your socials today?

**Marnie**    My brother Chris.

**Chris**    Er, Marn – I'm sure you know, but there appears to be a deepfake video of you all over the internet. The good news is . . . it's not porn.

**Marnie**    My mum – the only person who still leaves me voicemails. Oblivious.

*SFX: Voicemail notification.*

**Linda**   I hope you had a great holiday and you *remembered* to put suncream on my grandson (*Laughs.*). See you soon – *hopefully*. Safe flight!

*SFX: A ping.*

**Marnie**   A WhatsApp group I have no recollection of joining.

**Friend One**   Have you seen this? What a cow! Who speaks to her child like that?

**Friend Two**   Erm Jaz, I think that's Marnie?

*SFX: Notification.*

**Marnie**   'Jaz has left the group.'

(,)

I press play on one of the links titled 'Britain's Worst Mother?'

*SFX: We hear some audio of the altercation we saw earlier.*

**Marnie** *stops the video.*

Fuck fuck fuck.

(,)

I return to baggage reclaim. I watch Jake.

He's turning his phone back on.

I turn my phone off.

Put it in my pocket.

Pull out a crumpled packet of valium.

*She holds it up.*

Too. Fucking. Late.

(,)

I walk to my family. People stare.

I catch eyes with the girl from the plane. She looks down and scurries off.

Charlie runs to me.

Hugs my leg.

Holds me up.

Jake and I lock eyes.

He storms over, grasping his phone.

**Jake**    Marnie.

What the fuck have you done?


**Scene Four**

**Marnie**    The day after.

It's just like any other regular Sunday really.

You know – do the cleaning, do the washing, think of inventive ways to kill myself . . .

My husband avoids me.

My child clings to me.

It's suffocating.

I ignore voicemails from my mum.

*SFX: Voicemail notification.*

**Linda**    Marnie, your dad and I are worried sick. What have you done? Your brother said you've gone viral on Tick Tack!

**Marnie**    I go to the supermarket.

Spend an unreasonable amount of time staring at things in the bargain aisle.

I leave with our shopping, an air-fryer we'll never use and spit on my shoulder.

**Woman**    Stupid fucking bitch. Shouldn't have had kids

**Marnie**    Says the mother who is swearing at a stranger in front of *her* two kids.

(,)

I don't remember the drive home.

(,)

Jake and I eat in silence. I struggle to swallow.

**Jake**    I'll take him in tomorrow.

**Marnie**    No. It's his first day of school.

**Jake**    Marnie, do you understand what you've done? You called our son a –

**Marnie**    I know. *I was there.*

**Jake**    You should call the doctor's tomorrow.

**Marnie**    I *need t*o take my son to school. *I'm his mother.*

**Jake**    Then start acting like one.


**Scene Five**

**Marnie** *is holding* **Charlie***'s hand.*

**Marnie**    We're at the school gates.

This is *the* moment.

The moment you let go of their hand and . . .

I've been secretly looking forward to this for months.

I don't think you're supposed to say that though are you?

But I don't want to let go of his hand.

He looks scared.

I hold his face. Touch the freckles on his nose. Kiss his forehead.

We cling to each other.

*She looks up.*

I'm not good at small talk.

I'm awkward.

Some people assume 'awkward' is the same thing as 'aloof'.

Groups are forming. Introductions are made.

The seeds of new friendships.

Play dates.

PTA meetings.

Prosecco friends.

It's like looking through a window.

*She approaches someone.*

Hi, I'm Marnie, we met at their nursery. Sorry, I can't remember your name –

**Woman** (*abruptly*)    Come on, Rosie, let's get you in.

**Marnie** *watches the woman rush off.*

**Marnie**    Charlie is pointing.

**Charlie** (*pointing*)    Cunt. Cunt.

Coat.

**Marnie**    Coat? Coat!

He definitely said 'coat'.

Shit. I forgot his coat.

I am a terrible mother.

**Scene Six**

**Marnie**   I drive home. Check my phone.

My boss has messaged me.

*SFX: Message notification.*

**Joss**   Hi, Marnie, did you know that you've gone *virile*?

**Marnie**   I'm assuming that's a typo.

Joss is typing. Message deleted. Joss is typing.

*SFX: Message notification.*

**Joss**   Hi, Marnie – hope you had a great holiday! Sunshine emoji.

Sorry, but we've cancelled your hot yoga class today. You didn't have any bookings. Sad face emoji.

**Marnie**   Shit.

(,)

I open Google.

I search.

Refresh.

Search.

I've spread to other countries.

I am a virus.

A pandemic.

Germany.

North America.

Japan.

It's been trending all day in Australia.

Millions and millions and –

I throw up.

I feel dirty. Disgusting.

I run a bath.

I slide under the water . . . like they do in films when they need to show the character is depressed.

I take my phone with me.

*SFX: Phone splashing into the water.*

*She sighs.*

*SFX: Notification (underwater).*

Then I find out . . . that my phone is fucking waterproof.

(,)

They've found me.

'This is her. That bitch from the plane. @marnie-does-yoga.'

The replies are vicious. Violent. Vitriolic.

Apart from one.

**Girl**    I know this sounds weird, but does anyone know where she got that top from?

**Marnie**    I reply. Vinted.

I scroll.

**Various Voices** (*audio or live*)    What about the boy?

That poor boy!

He's the victim.

He doesn't stand a chance.

He'll have PTSD.

As a trauma therapist I'm concerned by –

It's emotional abuse.

I'm gonna call the NSPCC.

And the RSPCA.

Call the police.

Call social services.

Save the boy.

Save him.

Save the son!

**Marnie**    A hashtag is now trending.

Hashtag son-of-a-bitch.


**Scene Seven**

**Airport** (*V/O*)    Emirates Flight EK349 to London Heathrow is delayed due to severe weather conditions. Please wait for further announcements at Gate 13.

**Marnie**    A four-hour delay.

The gate is noisy, stuffy, packed.

Jake is off taking urgent work calls.

(*,*)

I'm very aware there's one valium left in my pocket.

The doctor only gave me two.

One for the flight here.

One for the way back.

(*,*)

I took Jake's seat. He sat with Charlie a few rows behind.

I slept. I read.

Seven hours of . . . space.

You see our flights had been booked separately.

**Jake**    I'm going to Dubai for the restructure conference. Come with me. We can have our first family holiday.

**Marnie**    I'd never been this far. Too scared to fly.

(,)

The holiday was . . . amazing.

I finally understood the Instagram pics.

*That's* what I'd signed up for.

Little footprints on the beach.

First splashes in the sea.

Giggles. Joy.

Charlie was . . . fine. Delightful.

It must have just been a phase.

When we got back he'd start school.

And I could work more.

**Charlie**    Plane! Mummy! Plane!

**Marnie**    That's right! Mummy take a picture?

**Jake**    Marnie – bit of a situation. They just called me over. I've been upgraded.

To business class.

**Marnie**    What? But what about us? He's not slept – he's going to be a –

**Jake**    Mine's a separate work booking so I can't change yours.

I did try. Flight is oversold – it's full.

And I've got *a lot* of work to do.

**Marnie**    Right.

**Jake**    You know it's called business class for a reason?

**Marnie**    Really? Thanks for explaining.

**Jake**    Sorry. Sorry. I'll swap with you when I'm done, OK?

(,)

**Marnie**    Is this about last night?

**Jake**    Look, we both said some things we didn't –

**Marnie** (*to audience*)    There's an announcement.

We're boarding.

I watch Jake turn left.


**Scene Eight**

**Marnie**    I was not an easy child. Apparently I was –

**Linda**    Stubborn. Selfish. Difficult.

**Colin**    Your mother's worried sick again, Marnie.

**Marnie**    Parents Northern.

She was a nurse. He was in the army, so we moved around a lot.

Settled in Aldershot.

Although I never felt . . . *settled*.

I had one friend. My older brother Chris.

**Linda**    You got the looks, Marnie, but your brother got the brains.

**Marnie**    The golden son. Annoyingly perfect.

(*She smiles.*) My best friend.

(,)

I failed exams.

Followed the crowd.

Followed a bad boyfriend to London.

Landed in Camden in the noughties.

Worked in pubs, offices, lettings, marketing.

Everything felt transient.

Fast. Fleeting.

Fearless.

I couldn't *commit* to *anything.*

I moved in with a girl called Lucy whose parents had brought her a flat.

**Lucy**   You can have the attic room. Do you like coke? Do you have an eating disorder? It's fine if you do. I was bulimic through most of the nineties.

**Marnie**   She wafted round the flat with a fag in her mouth, and an incense stick in her bun.

I'd *never* met anyone like her.

She was exotic. Properly posh.

And she *adored* me.

**Lucy**   We're going to have so much fun! I can tell.

Bin the boyfriend though, Marnie. He's *very* generic.

**Marnie**   I didn't have to. He dumped me.

**Lucy**   What a cock. Never mind. Let's go to the pub and stalk Amy Winehouse.

**Marnie**   Festivals, noisy pubs, new friends.

We partied.

Got fucked.

Got laid.

I got pregnant.

**Lucy**    Oh fuck. Fuck!

Don't worry, I've had two abortions.

I mean, you can't keep it. It'll ruin your life.

(,)

Do you know what the world's biggest sexually transmitted disease is, Marnie?

Children.

**Marnie**    I have an abortion. Lucy comes with me.

(*To* **Lucy**.) What if I . . . regret *not* having it?

**Lucy**    What if you regret *having it*?

(,)

**Marnie**    Life slows down. Shifts. We start going to weddings.

**Lucy**    Well I'm *never* getting married. It's so fucking generic.

(,)

**Marnie**    But she did, they *all* did.

Settle. Down.

**Lucy**    He's called Josh. I'm obsessed.

If I'm not engaged by thirty I'll kill myself.

**Marnie**    I became the girl you *live with*, before you find a husband.

**Linda**    And the girl men date before they find a wife.

**Marnie**    I was Samantha Jones.

**Lucy**    No no wait – you're Bridget Jones.

**Marnie**    For other people's amusement.

**Lucy**    Marnie, tell us about your latest disastrous date!

(*To a waiter.*) Four Cosmopolitans please.

God, I love this. You're hilarious. She's hilarious!

**Marnie**    I go to a lot of weddings.

Alone.

My diary begins to empty as they migrate to the suburbs.

They talk about mortgages.

Extensions.

Garden furniture.

The cost of childcare.

Calpol.

Costco.

I have nothing to add.

(,)

New flatmates. New jobs. New boyfriends.

New questions like –

**Nosey Woman**    Do you have kids?

**Marnie**    Because if you're not a mother by a certain age, people assume –

**Nosey Woman**    You're one of those high-powered career women who doesn't like kids?

**Marnie**    I am totally lost.

I have no idea what I actually *want*.

I am not a wife. Or a mother.

I haven't climbed a ladder or smashed a glass ceiling.

(,)

My brother meets someone.

**Chris**   His name's Robert.

**Linda**   Oh, Marnie, I don't care that he's gay. I'm just upset that I'll *never* have grandchildren now.

**Marnie**   Erm – I'm not dead.

**Linda**   You said you didn't want any.

**Marnie**   I don't.

**Linda**   You'll change your mind when you meet someone. Won't she, Colin?

**Colin**   She could try that new dating application. Tinder! It's very good.

**Linda**   Oh yes, that's a good idea.

(,)

(*Suspicious.*) How do *you* know?


**Scene Nine**

*SFX: Plane engine noise.*

**Pilot** (*V/O*)   Cabin crew prepare for take-off.

**Marnie**   I'm crammed into the middle seat.

Charlie is on my left, playing a game on the iPad.

There's a tall girl to my right. Asleep. She smells of *all* the perfume testers.

**Cabin Crew** (*V/O*)   Should the cabin experience sudden pressure loss, oxygen masks will drop down from above your seat.

**Marnie** *searches her pocket.*

**Marnie**   I can't find the valium.

**Cabin Crew** (*V/O*)   Place the mask over your mouth and nose. Pull the strap to tighten it.

**Marnie** (*panicking*)    It's not in my pockets. My bag?

(*She turns to* **Charlie**.) Stop it.

(*To audience.*) It's gone.

**Cabin Crew** (*V/O*)    If you are travelling with children, make sure that your own mask is on first before helping them with theirs.

**Marnie** (*to* **Charlie**)    Sit still!

(,)

Yep.

(*To audience.*) I'll definitely put my mask on first.

(,)

We ascend.

*She closes her eyes and grips onto the seat.*

*SFX: Plane engine noise increases as they take off.*


**Scene Ten**

**Marnie**    For the first time in my life I've been single for more than six months.

I'm fine with it.

But nobody else is.

**Lucy**    Marnie, do you want me to set you up with my friend Hugo? He's loaded.

Though he's what I call a bit of a prawn – great body, weak face.

**Linda**    Christine's daughter met someone on Guardian Soulmates! She's pregnant now – isn't she, Colin?

**Colin**    Oh. I thought she was just plump.

**Marnie**    I try Guardian Soulmates. There are some decent men in their forties, but they're mostly like –

**Man**    Mark, forty-six. Looking for a woman aged between twenty-two and thirty-four.

**Marnie**    I'm thirty-five.

**Linda**    The age when your fertility falls off a cliff, Marnie.

**Marnie**    I'm thirty-five and sharing a fridge with three people.

I'm about to give up and then I meet –

**Jake**    Jake. Forty-two. Work in tech, but I'm not boring. I wear odd socks.

I like true crime podcasts but I'm not a serial killer.

I look like a really crap Ryan Gosling tribute act.

Looking for someone to share life with.

**Marnie**    I'm expecting to be underwhelmed. Or rejected.

But he's lovely. Shy. Endearing.

**Jake**    My dad died when I was a kid and Mum is in a care home now. Dementia.

They had me in their forties after being told they were infertile.

I was a bit of a miracle really.

Like a shit Jesus.

**Marnie**    We can't stop laughing. Can't stop talking.

No ambiguity. No games.

**Jake**    I know you can't have a cat in your flat so I got you a toy one.

Actually I got two. A ginger one and a black one because I panicked.

**Marnie**   He's got his own flat. On date three we don't leave it for seventy-two hours.

**Linda**   He's lovely, Marnie. We love him. Don't mess it up.

**Marnie**   I am *not* going to mess this up.

I will be . . . whatever he wants me to be.

**Jake**   So, Marnie . . . what do you want?

**Marnie**   Want?

**Jake**   Like . . . in the future. Any dreams?

**Marnie**   Oh. Erm – find a job I actually like . . . Get a *real* cat. You?

**Jake**   Umm, travel. Sell the flat, buy a house, have a family . . .

With you. *With you*, Marnie.

I know it sounds a bit Deepak Chopra, but I think I manifested you.

**Marnie**   He proposes.

I am giddy with happiness.

I must tell everyone.

I must take a photo.

I must tell my mum.

(,)

Things happen quickly at that age.

Move in, get married.

Tick box. Tick box.

Tick tock.

**Jake**   Let's start trying.

**Marnie**    Woah! Can't we just enjoy being married for a bit first? Just the two of us?

**Jake**    Imagine when there's three of us. Our little family.

You'll be such a great mum, Marnie.

You do want that, don't you?

**Marnie**    Yes. Yes of course . . . I mean, it's a big thing . . . I just haven't –

**Jake**    We should try soon though.

If we want two.

**Marnie**    We want two?

**Jake**    Because of your age – I mean you don't – *we* don't . . . have much time.

**Linda**    Apparently, Marnie, lots of women are now freezing their eggs. I read it in the *Daily Mail*, didn't I, Colin?

**Colin**    In the freezer? We wouldn't have room in ours, it's packed!

**Marnie**    Jake, can't we just freeze them – my eggs?

**Jake**    Why? We've got no reason to wait, have we?

You don't even like your job.


**Scene Eleven**

*SFX: Plane engine noise.*

**Marnie**    Charlie, stop banging the tray. Stop it. You're going to –

(*To the passenger in front.*) Sorry. I'm so sorry!

(*To* **Charlie**.) Say sorry to the lady. Say sorry.

(,)

He's sorry.

(,)

*Stop* making that noise

(*To the passenger next to her.*) I'm so sorry about this.

**Air Hostess**   Any drinks, snacks?

**Marnie**   Can I get another red wine please?

Actually make that two. He threw the first one I had all over me.

**Air Hostess**   Awww, I'm sure it was an accident.

**Marnie**   It wasn't.

**Air Hostess**   And for the boy?

**Marnie**   Just a double vodka, please!

**Air Hostess** *doesn't laugh.*

(,)

**Marnie**   I'm joking. Just an apple juice.

**Air Hostess**   How old are you? Four! Wow! What a lovely age.

**Marnie**   Not really.

How long have we got left on the flight?

**Air Hostess**   Five hours.

**Marnie**   Do you still do that thing where kids can sit with the pilot in the cockpit . . . for the majority of the flight?

**Air Hostess**   That was never a thing.

**Marnie** (*to audience*)   This is the moment things really go to shit.

*She turns to* **Charlie** *and her eyes widen.*

**Marnie**   The iPad runs out of battery.

(,)

I brace for impact.

**Scene Twelve**

**Marnie**    On Charlie's third day of school I give up. Jake takes him in.

I make a doctor's appointment.

My brother Chris comes round.

We watch a feature on a morning TV show. About me.

**Chris**    God, they're desperate for content. It's because it's August.

It's what journalists call 'the silly season'.

Next time you call Charlie a cunt, make sure you do it in winter.

**Marnie**    A presenter stands next to the creepy mannequin of a small child.

**Presenter**    I'm joined by Julia McKenzie, author of *The Gentle Parenting Guide.*

So, Julia, how *should* parents react when a child is provoking a reaction?

**Julia**    Body language is crucial. Raising your voice is only going to make the problem worse.

**Chris**    Wow. What a fucking revelation.

**Julia**    Kneel down so you are at their height – like a friend. Hold their hands.

**Chris**    I'm really worried she's going to pull those hands off. They're *very* wobbly.

(*Doing impression.*) If you accidentally rip your child's hands off, it's going to make the problem worse!

**Julia**   Let's do some belly breaths and tummy pats together –

**Chris**   Oh fuck off, Julia.

**Marnie**   We've got her book.

It's one of many self-help books I own which DIDN'T FUCKING HELP.

(,)

Do you think I'm a shit mother?

(,)

**Chris**   Yes.

I mean you probably are. Sometimes.

And sometimes you're probably brilliant.

(,)

Isn't that what parenting is?


**Scene Thirteen**

**Marnie**   After the honeymoon, we start trying.

**Jake**   Marn, I've brought you some more ovulation sticks.

**Linda**   You need to just relax, Marnie! It'll happen when you relax.

**Marnie**   The more people told me that – to *relax* – the *less* relaxed I felt.

Lots of sex.

Unsexy sex.

My orgasm is *not* the priority.

**Linda**   Any news, love?

**Marnie**   Tests, lots of tests.

Tick tock.

Tick tock

Results.

**Consultant**    I'm sorry but you have a very low ovarian egg reserve. Your best bet is IVF.

You're entitled to one round on the NHS.

**Jake**    We'll do it. We'll do anything, won't we, Marn?

**Marnie**    Injections. Hormones.

Excitement. Disappointment.

**Jake**    We'll try again. Your body is just getting used to it.

**Marnie**    But how will we afford to pay?

**Linda**    We'll pay. Your dad and I will pay, Marnie. We *insist*.

**Marnie**    I'm on the fertility train now.

It's addictive.

A hope factory.

Success stories all over the walls.

Cards and pictures sent to consultants. Arranged to be in our eyeline. We want to be *one of them*.

You never hear about the failures.

They become invisible.

Hiding in the shadows of their own grief.

(,)

Round two doesn't work.

We keep going.

Can't stop now.

Round three.

Round three works but . . .

(,)

Quiet.

Early.

Jake is . . . distanced.

I am. Numb. Empty.

I am . . .

**Jake**    We'll try again. Whenever you're ready.

**Marnie**    I ask for space.

Life continues.

I'm trying not to fall.

Yoga catches me.

I retrain as a yoga teacher.

(*She smiles.*) I begin to feel . . .

Jake gets me a cat. A ginger one.

A tiny little thing. A rescue.

It's as broken as me.

We heal each other.

(,)

And among the grief, there is relief.

The two are entwined.

And it fucks with my head.

**Jake**    I think we should try again, Marnie.

**Consultant**    You may need to explore other options now. Have you considered a donor egg?

**Scene Fourteen**

*SFX: Plane engine noise.*

**Marnie**   Charlie is smacking the iPad.

**Charlie**   It's broken. Broken!

**Marnie**   Shall we pick a film on the TV instead?

**Charlie**   No! Want game! Want Daddy!

**Marnie**   I get a nudge, and a waft of perfume.

**Ella**   Here, have my power pack.

Looks like you need it more than me.

**Marnie**   Thank you.

Look, Charlie. Say thank you to the nice lady.

Say thank you. Ow! (*She snatches her hand away.*)

(*To **Ella**.*) Sorry, he's tired. Thank you.

(*To audience.*) She's pretty. Late twenties. Beachy hair. Tanned. Lots of bracelets. Relaxed.

I fucking hate her.

**Ella**   No worries. You look like you need a break.

**Marnie**   We just had one. A holiday I mean.

**Ella**   Me too. Kind of. Very long one. Been travelling for ten months.

I'm Ella.

**Marnie**   I'm Marnie

(*To audience.*) I notice Ella grimace at Charlie. He's got snot hanging out of his nose.

(*To **Ella**, laughing.*) Oh the joys of parenthood.

**Ella**   I don't know how you do it.

**Marnie**    Well it's –

**Ella**    Different when it's your own?

**Marnie** (*laughs*)    Yeah.

No. No it's not. That's bullshit.

**Ella**    Must be hard doing it alone though.

**Marnie**    Oh I'm not alone – my husband's in business class.

I am aware that sounds weird.

His flights were booked separately by his company. He's been upgraded.

He's doing some *very* important work.

(,)

Do you want another . . . gin? I don't normally drink much. Bit of a nervous flyer. Sorry I'm – I'm waffling.

(*To audience*.) We drink. We talk.

She's lovely. Funny. She reminds me of – *before*.

(*To* **Ella**.) Did you ever get lonely? Travelling by yourself.

**Ella**    No. (*Laughs*.) I was never really alone though.

Unless I *chose* to be.

**Marnie** (*to audience*)    I think about choices.

What if I made the wrong ones?

Is that what a midlife crisis is?

Grieving the paths we didn't take.

The people we could've been.

Compare. And despair.

(,)

(*To* **Ella**.) So, Ella, why has your trip finished?

**Ella**    Duty calls. My mother. She's dying.

**Marnie**    Oh god, I'm so sorry.

**Ella**    No, don't be.

She's an absolute bitch.

But hey – she's still my mother.


**Scene Fifteen**

**Marnie**    It's my thirty-eighth birthday. We're in PizzaExpress, with my parents.

**Jake**    We're thinking of getting a donor egg.

**Linda**    What's wrong with *her* eggs?

**Marnie**    The doctor says we'll have more of a chance with a donor egg.

**Colin**    How do they get them out? The eggs? I know how they do it with the men – you know – the cup and the . . . the magazines.

**Marnie**    I don't know, Dad. I can't get my head around any of it – I mean it wouldn't be . . . *mine*.

**Jake**    It would still be *ours*, Marnie. It doesn't matter where it came from.

**Linda**    Well I'm sorry, but of course it does. What if it's a psychopath with bad genes? What if it's ugly? *She's* got a lovely face!

**Marnie**    Mum, you're not helping! It's just like . . . you'd be having a baby with another woman. A stranger. And I'd be . . . carrying it.

**Linda**    At least it would have *your* genes, Jake. It would be very calm.

(,)

**Marnie**    I look at my dad. He's staring at his menu.

**Colin**    I think I might change my order. I don't think I want the Fiorentina anymore. It's got an egg on it.

## Scene Sixteen

**Marnie**    Eight months later I'm pregnant.

I feel serene.

Powerful.

I feel.

Seen.

(,)

I wear the tightest clothes.

Rub my belly.

Get my 'baby on board' badge.

I am about to join the club.

Belong.

Have a purpose.

A reason.

An answer.

'What do you do?'

I. Am. A. Mother.

## Scene Seventeen

**Marnie**    After the twenty-week scan Jake says –

**Jake**    We need to sell the flat and leave the city.

**Marnie**    But I'm settled here. It's right near the station.

**Jake**    We'll get you a car!

**Marnie** (*to audience*)    I fucking *hate* driving.

**Jake**    This flat is tiny. We need at least three bedrooms and a garden.

**Marnie** (*to audience*)    We look at houses in small towns that all look the same.

**Jake** *walks around pointing at things.*

**Jake**    This garden is not big enough.

That's a box room.

There's no electric car charging point.

**Marnie**    The houses get further away. And some don't exist at all.

**Estate Agent**    That was just the show home of course, but you can see the potential.

This would be your plot here. Overlooking these fields.

**Marnie**    There's nothing for miles around.

It's flat.

Exposed.

Windy.

Quiet . . . *Eerily* quiet.

**Jake**    I know it's more remote than we wanted, but the schools are amazing.

This will be a new start, Marnie. An adventure!

**Marnie**    There's a delay with the building work so we remain in the flat.

(,)

Then suddenly.

He's here.

**Linda**    Oh, Marnie! He's the *best* thing that's ever happened to me.

(,)

**Marnie**    I make friends in baby groups.

Walk for hours with Charlie strapped to me.

We are like one person.

(,)

Some people say the beginning is the hardest bit.

But I *loved* the beginning.

I *loved* being a mum.

Until he started to get a personality.

(,)

It turns out Charlie is allergic to the cat.

My cat.

**Jake**    We have to get rid of him.

(,)

The cat. Not Charlie.

(,)

I am grief stricken. It floors me.

I cry for days. Can't eat.

Jake thinks I'm being ridiculous.

**Jake**    It's just a cat, Marnie.

**Marnie**    But I *always wanted* a cat.

(,)

Then suddenly the new house is ready.

I don't have time to think about it.

We're moving. We move.

Then lockdown happens.

And we're fucked.

**Scene Eighteen**

*SFX: Plane engine noise.*

**Cabin Crew** (*V/O*)  Ladies and gentlemen, we will now be dimming the lights for your comfort.

**Marnie** (*to* **Charlie**)  Mummy needs you to sit quietly now.

Shall we try that film again?

*SFX: Turbulence.*

**Pilot** (*V/O*)  Ladies and gentlemen, we are experiencing a little turbulence. Please remain in your seats and fasten your seatbelt.

**Marnie** (*to* **Charlie**)  Stop. That. Now.

(*To passenger in front.*) So sorry! He's just a nervous flyer.

(*To* **Charlie**.) Charlie, the lady is getting very cross and needs you to stop kicking her seat.

(*To passenger in front.*) Yes, I'm aware it's a night flight.

No, I don't think he's grasped that yet, he's only four.

Well maybe if you hadn't reclined your seat in the first five minutes of the flight we'd actually have some space –

**Jake**  Marnie . . . is everything OK?

**Marnie**  Oh. Hello, stranger.

**Jake**  Have you been drinking? Marnie, you shouldn't be drinking if you're – you *shouldn't* be drinking.

**Marnie**    Are you done? With your *important* work?

*SFX: Turbulence.*

**Air Hostess**    Sir, I'm going to have to ask you to go back to your seat and leave the boy with the nanny.

**Marnie**    Nanny? You think I'm his fucking nanny – *I'm his mother!*

**Jake**    Marnie, calm down.

(*To* **Air Hostess**.) I'm so sorry, I'll go back.

She is actually his moth– I'm on a business trip so I erm – never mind.

*SFX: Turbulence.*

**Marnie** (*to* **Charlie**)    Mummy needs you to put your seatbelt on now . . . sorry

Mummy help? (*She fastens his seatbelt.*) Good boy.

Don't be scared. It's just the clouds making it bounce.

Don't be scared. Everything is going to be OK.

*SFX: Turbulence.*


**Scene Nineteen**

**Marnie**    During lockdown, Jake works from home.

He buys a headset.

**Jake** (*shouting*)    OK, let's all regroup.

Yeah, sure – EOP tomorrow?

Can you unmute yourself, Richard?

You're on mute, mate. You're on mute.

**Marnie**    For a new house, it's surprisingly noisy.

Hollow walls. Wonky plugs.

It's either too cold. Or too hot.

Charlie is as loud as his annoying toys.

**Toy Voice** (*high pitched*)   Do you know your ABC? Well done!

Can you find the shape?

**Charlie**   Peppa! Mama! Peppa!

**Marnie**   I want to slaughter Peppa Pig and put her in a bacon sandwich.

Charlie hasn't learnt to mix.

He's scared of going out.

We both are now.

(,)

Then suddenly it's over.

Masks off.

Jake is back to work. Out all day.

'Back to normal.'

Although it's not.

Normal.

None of it.

I get a car. I fucking hate driving. I'm a nervous wreck.

When he's at nursery I miss him, but I also don't want him to come home yet.

I don't understand. Is that normal?

I don't know who to ask.

(,)

Sometimes I feel like he's a lodger and not my son.

Someone is going to turn up at the door and say 'Thank you for looking after him, we'll take him now'.

The only thing he likes is soft play.

Have you ever been to soft play?

It's hell.

(,)

Everyone's on WhatsApp now.

I lose track.

Lose friends.

Lose things.

Including my temper.


**Scene Twenty**

**Marnie**    When Charlie hits 'the terrible twos', my mum comes to stay.

**Linda**    Where's my gorgeous grandson?

**Marnie**    She *adores* him.

For the first time in my life – *I'm* the favourite one.

I bombard the family WhatsApp group with pictures of my son.

Chris's latest achievement – partner at his law firm – gets lost among videos of Charlie's milestones.

**Linda**    What are those marks on your arm?

(*Concerned.*) Have you been?

You haven't been . . . again?

**Marnie**    No, it was Charlie.

**Linda** (*laughing*)    You need to cut his nails!

**Marnie**   And remove his teeth?

(,)

**Linda**   He's a good kid, Marnie.

**Marnie**   Yeah, in front of you. When he's with me he's –

**Linda**   *He's just a child.* Toddlers are hard work.

(*Scoffs.*) I knew this would happen.

**Marnie**   What's that supposed to mean?

**Linda**   Getting bored of something as soon as you've got it. Never satisfied.

**Marnie**   That's not fair, it's –

**Linda**   It's because you all leave it so late.

In my day there was no time to mess about.

You got married, had kids, worked hard.

Nothing to compare it to.

*Your* generation is spoilt and selfish. Entitled.

**Marnie**   Oh, well I can never do anything right, can I?

**Linda**   Stop playing the victim. You *wanted* this.

**Marnie**   No, *you* wanted this.

**Linda**   *Stop* blaming everyone else!

(,)

**Marnie**   I'm sorry. It's just I – I'm really –

**Linda** (*pointing*)   What's that hole in the wall?

**Marnie**   Oh, that was . . . that was Charlie. He kicked a hole in the wall.

(,)

If you could do it all over again – have kids. Would you?

**Linda**    If I had the choices you do?

(,)

No.


**Scene Twenty-One**

**Marnie** (*to audience*)    A few days before the holiday, I call Lucy.

(*To* **Lucy**.) I think I might be pregnant.

(,)

**Lucy**    And it might not be Jake's?

**Marnie**    Why would it *not be* Jake's?

**Lucy**    Oh! You're still fucking your own husband? Lucky you!

**Marnie**    I've got the same symptoms as before – late period, sore boobs.

I'm moody – *really moody* –

**Lucy**    We're all moody, darling, it's called being middle aged.

**Marnie**    I just got a test from Boots. She winked at me and said 'good luck'.

**Lucy**    What a presumptuous bitch!

**Marnie**    Why does everyone assume you want it to be positive?

(,)

**Lucy**    Do you *want it* to be positive?

**Marnie**    No.

I don't know.

I'm scared.

**Lucy**   You should be. Two can be a fucking nightmare.

Even with an au pair.

(,)

What does Jake say?

**Marnie**   Have you ever been on that Facebook page 'I Regret Having Children'?

**Lucy**   No. (*She laughs.*) That sounds hilarious.

(,)

**Marnie**   Do you ever . . . wish you'd . . . do you ever regret –

**Lucy**   Marnie, everyone regrets having children sometimes.

It's a fucking ballache.

(,)

Charlie is just being a little prick.

*All children* go through that phase.

He'll grow out of it.

*Then* you'll see how fucking amazing it can be.

(,)

Marnie, are you OK?

**Marnie** (*to audience*)   I put the test away.


**Scene Twenty-Two**

**Marnie**   It's half term. Six weeks after the video.

Jake's taken Charlie camping. It's their first trip alone.

I'm at Chris's in Brighton. We take his dogs for a walk on the beach.

**Chris**   Have you thought about taking him for tests?

**Marnie**   We did. Before the holiday. They said there was nothing wrong.

**Chris**   So he's not got – like one of the things beginning with A?

**Marnie**   No.

**Chris**   So *he is* just a little cunt.

(,)

**Marnie**   I bet you're relieved.

**Chris**   Relieved?

**Marnie**   That you've got dogs not kids. You chose wisely.

**Chris**   Chose? You think I *chose* not to have children?

**Marnie**   You never wanted them. You –

**Chris**   Did you even bother to ask me what I wanted? Did everyone just assume that just because I was gay I was done with the idea of kids?

**Marnie**   Sorry, I just . . . assumed you –

**Chris**   It's easier now, there are more options – but back then . . .

I did my grieving a long time ago. Alone.

**Marnie**   I'm sorry. I didn't realise you wanted –

**Chris**   I don't. Not now.

I had the space to *really* think about it.

That was a gift. That space.

Because it's the biggest thing you can ever do. Raise a human.

Not just *a baby*.

In *this* world. This shitty little world.

**Marnie**    I thought it would make me feel – that it would . . .

I've never felt so alone.

**Chris**    Neither choice is easy.

Neither choice is *better*.

Some people don't get a choice.

(,)

**Marnie**    Sorry, I'm trying. I'm trying to be – I'm trying to fix it . . . Sorry.

**Chris**    Stop saying sorry.

**Marnie** (*crying*)    Sorry. Sorry. Sorry.

(,)

**Chris**    Do you remember what Great Auntie Niamh used to say? Granny's sister?

**Marnie**    Fuck yeah . . . Great Auntie Niamh.

**Chris** (*Irish accent*)    Don't have kids. Have animals.

Puppies become dogs.

Kittens become cats.

And children become cunts.

(*They laugh.*)

**Marnie** (*to audience*)    Jake calls. They've had to come home from camping.

Because Charlie has bitten another kid and is being 'a little shit'.

His words, not mine.

His words.

He is struggling to cope.

He's not sure what he's doing wrong.

He sounds . . . hysterical.

(,)

(*Smirking.*) I tell him to calm down.


**Scene Twenty-Three**

**Marnie**    The evening before the flight home.

Twenty-four hours before over ten million people see the worst moment of my life.

Jake and I have dinner in comfortable silence.

We've had a lovely day. Our little family. The three of us.

I still haven't done the test.

**Jake**    Are we OK? I just wanted to say I'm sorry things have been – that I've not been very . . . present. At home.

**Marnie**    OK.

**Jake**    Work has been . . . I feel really pressured. I want to be at home more.

**Marnie**    OK . . . I – I think I've just felt –

**Jake**    I think we should try again. For another baby.

(,)

**Marnie**    I erm –

**Jake**    I think Charlie should have a sibling. For when we're not around any more.

I know what you're thinking, but it's not *impossible* – I've already spoken to the consultant we had before.

**Marnie**    You've done *what*?

**Jake**    Sorry, I know I probably shouldn't have but I –

**Marnie**    Then why the fuck did you then?

**Jake**    Marnie, keep your voice down. Our son is asleep.

**Marnie**    Our son? *Our* son? I'm very aware we have a son, Jake.

I was the one who was pressured into having him.

(,)

**Jake**    You were not pressured into having him.

**Marnie**    Yes I was.

Not just by you.

From the moment *my* mum gave me dolls to play mummy with, so I could be just like her. Just like every other woman.

'How many kids do you want?'

'Why haven't you got kids?'

'Oh you're married now! So when are you having kids'?

**Jake**    Look I know we've been through a tough time but –

**Marnie**    We? *We?*

It's was me who was . . . it was – *my* body –

The . . . the miscarriage.

That didn't even affect you.

All you cared about was trying again.

(,)

**Jake**    I was devastated, Marnie. Devastated.

I didn't know how to . . .

I was trying to be strong for you.

**Marnie**    I felt so alone.

(,)

**Jake**   I don't understand.

I've given you a nice home, a nice life.

You have both parents – your brother.

I have nothing.

My own mum doesn't know who I am anymore.

I've tried to be a good husband.

**Marnie**   I don't think you manifested me.

**Jake**   What?

**Marnie**   I think you just wanted a wife.

**Jake**   No, I wanted you. *You*, Marnie.

**Marnie** (*sarcastic*)   Well that turned out well for you.

**Jake**   You're impossible.

**Marnie**   Can you not hear me? *Can anybody hear me?*

**Jake**   Marnie, calm down –

**Marnie** (*shouting*)   I fucking hate being a mother. I fucking hate it.

And he knows.

He knows.

Because *he hates me.*

And sometimes.

I. Hate. Him.

**Jake**   Please don't say that. Please.

**Marnie**   I think I'm pregnant.

(,)

**Jake**   What? Why didn't you tell me?

(,)

**Marnie**   Because you'll want me to keep it.

## Scene Twenty-Four

*SFX: Plane engine noise.*

**Ella**   Are you OK?

**Marnie**   Yeah – sorry I woke you, Ella.

**Ella**   Was that your husband?

**Marnie**   Yeah.

**Ella**   Right. I recognise him.

From the desk at the gate.

When I was asking about the delays.

He asked to be upgraded.

**Marnie**   Sorry?

**Ella**   He asked to be upgraded. They didn't call him over.

He didn't mention he was with his family.

(,)

**Marnie**   Right.

## Scene Twenty-Five

**Marnie**   I'm finally at the doctor's.

I feel sick.

She's frowning.

Though she's also casually nibbling on a packet of Quavers, so I'm assuming I don't have cancer.

**Doctor**   Right, well you're definitely not pregnant.

**Marnie**   But my period hasn't –

**Doctor**    Perimenopause.

**Marnie**    What?

**Doctor**    It can mimic pregnancy. Which is weird when your body is basically doing the opposite.

**Marnie**    But I haven't had any hot flashes.

**Doctor**    Not everyone does. There are over forty symptoms

You might get those later on though. Fun!

**Marnie**    But I'm only forty-three.

**Doctor**    Yeah, it's not uncommon. Mine started at forty-one.

**Marnie**    Does it . . . can it affect your – moods?

**Doctor**    Oh Christ yes! Crying fits, anxiety, mood swings –

**Marnie**    Mood swings? Like you can suddenly get – *really* angry?

**Doctor**    The hot rage?

Throwing a remote control at your husband's head because he accidentally shrank your favourite jumper in the wash?

Yes.

It's like PMT.

On acid.


**Scene Twenty-Six**

**Marnie**    Two months after the video.

My job is gone. My marriage is fucked.

It's Jake who mentions the words 'trial separation'.

**Jake**    We should discuss custody. *If* we go down that road. And what's best for Charlie.

**Marnie**    Social services get in touch.

Apparently they've received 'a number of concerning reports'.

From the public? From my own husband?

The thought of my son being taken away from me is . . .

**Linda**   Awful . . . this is just awful.

When are they coming?

I'll bake bread.

The smell of bread. That's what they say to do.

**Colin**   I think that's estate agents, Linda. When you're trying to sell a house.

I don't think bread is going to help.

**Lucy**   What a bunch of pricks. Don't let them in.

**Marnie**   But I do.

There are two of them. They sit opposite me on the sofa.

Charlie is on his best behaviour.

(,)

Angelic.


**Scene Twenty-Seven**

Seven words. Ten seconds.

(,)

Did you enjoy it?

Did you share it?

Did it make you feel like a better person?

(,)

'Maybe she was drunk.'

'Maybe she's mad.'

'Or just a bitch.'

'Or a bad mother.'

And yes, *I am* his mother. He is *my* son.

Biologically.

No donor egg.

There is nobody else to blame.

(,)

We got pregnant naturally in the end.

When we stopped trying.

When I was . . . relaxed.

In that space.

The space between grief. And relief.

(,)

At fifteen weeks we announced it on social media.

I'm pregnant! We're pregnant!

**Various Voices** (*audio or live*)    Congratulations!

Welcome to the club!

You really deserve it.

Best feeling in the world.

You're gonna be an amazing mum.

You never know real love, until you've had a baby.

**Marnie**    Six hundred likes. One hundred comments. The most I've ever had.

For just having sex.

Without contraception.

(,)

Seven words. Ten seconds.

*You* can't press rewind and see what happened before.

Or press forward, and see what happened after.

I can.

In my head.

And I do.

Again and again.

And again.


**Scene Twenty-Eight**

*SFX: Plane engine noise.*

**Marnie**    I take Charlie to business class with me.

Jake *is* busy.

Drinking champagne and watching a film.

**Jake**    Marnie! I was just having a break – is everything – *are you drunk?*

**Marnie**    Are you working?

**Air Hostess**    Can I help you?

**Marnie**    Hi! I'm the nanny.

**Air Hostess**    I'm afraid you'll have to go back to your seat now.

**Marnie**    No thank you.

**Jake**    Sorry about this, Laura.

**Marnie**    Laura? What the fuck?

I'm getting kicked by a toddler while you drink Moet and flirt with Laura?

Well fuck this.

(*To audience.*) I grab his champagne and down it.

*SFX: Turbulence.*

I drop it.

**Jake**  Marnie, calm down.

**Air Hostess** (*reaches out her hand*)    I *really* need you to go back to your seat now.

**Marnie** (*smacks her hand away*)    Fuck off.

Hands grab me.

I am bulldozed back towards economy.

I fall through the curtain.

That's where the video starts.

(,)

I can hear Charlie crying.

I am pushed. I pull.

People staring.

Charlie is pulling at my leg now.

Pinching. Biting. Crying.

Jake keeps apologising. *To the crew.*

*SFX: Plane engine noise builds to a screeching crescendo.*

Charlie screams.

I explode.

(*Shouting.*) Shut the fuck up you little cunt.

(,)

There's an audible gasp.

I'm not sure if that's come from me.

Or my audience.

(,)

I look up.

Jake is frozen. Staring.

I try to find Ella.

She's standing up. Filming me on her phone.

(,)

That's where the video stops.

(,)

Fair play.

It's a strong ending.

*She falls to her knees and holds* **Charlie***'s face.*

**Marnie**   I'm sorry. I'm so so sorry.

I love you so much.

So so much. I'm so sorry.

Mummy is having a bad day.

I love you. I love you.

I'm so sorry.

(,)

*She slowly stands up – facing the audience.*

We cling to each other.

We are like one person.

I hold my breath.

Expect oxygen masks to drop from the ceiling.

But they don't.

(')

If they did, I would put his mask on first, before mine.

Every.

Single.

Time.

**Pilot** (V/O)   Cabin crew prepare for landing.

**Marnie**   They descend.

I fall.

*She looks down – reaches for **Charlie's** hand. Looks back up.*

**Marnie**   We fall.

(')

*She takes a deep breath in.*

*Blackout.*